If My Heart Could Talk & Other Poems

David Sanford

DEDICATION

To my mom and dad for supporting and believing in me.
To my sister for taking care of me and making me laugh.
To my aunt for helping me find the words.
To my Doctor, Frank Midgley, for saving my life.

FACING YOU WITH YOUR BROKEN HEART

Please, can you listen?
I know we're both hurt
You're in pain, and I have myself to blame
You're hiding within yourself,
But it's me who's scared

Facing you with your broken heart,
I have everything to lose

I can't ignore the ache in your voice
You plead for answers I don't yet have
I spend my days trying to find them

I'm sorry
I'm so sorry
Just tell me, how I can fix this?
Nothing can get better if we don't talk
I promise the scars will heal

GRAVITY

Walking down the street,
All the noises fade but the image of you catches my eye

I can't look away
Anchored in one spot,
I can't move

You don't know what I'm feeling

As you get closer,
I long for a sign of recognition
But there is none

Once you pass me,
The noises come back

I continue down the street
The connection is gone,
However the feeling stays

TRUST

I had doubts
I had fears
There's so much I want to explore about love

You came along
I reach for your hand, not knowing what to expect

Love is a risk

Trust can be beautiful
Trust can be dangerous
Do I need to trust you to love you?

CO-EXIST

Two people, like cars, can be headed in the same direction
Separated by distance and miles or traveling side by side
Stretch of highways for a long journey

Then one wonders,
Will they move ahead while the other is left behind?
No longer parallel
They just co-exist

Are they moving forward?
Will they be on the same road?
Or will one of them take a detour?
It's a choice that will affect each of them

Catch up
They want to reach their destination together

3 MONTHS

When I got the news,
I wanted time to stop
There was nothing I could do
I was angry
I was sad
I was hoping something would change
I said to myself this is it,
You've got to get through this

I used to believe time was on our side
That our lives were right on track
But once we waste a second,
We can't get it back

I questioned myself on so many things
I was afraid of death
Afraid of the future

3 months, and I'm still here
3 months, and I'm still breathing air

I'm fighting the fight
When I beat this,
I'll close the door,
But keep the memory of my strength

TEMPTATION

Alcohol is magic in liquid form

My mind was a jigsaw puzzle of a thousand pieces
Trying to make sense of the world,
The picture wasn't clear,
And I needed an escape

People drink every day
In restaurants, parties, church, home
Temptation was ever present
I would love to forget and be numb
A chance to ease my broken heart
A chance to forget all,
Even if it was temporary
Would it bring peace?

Yet, I have never indulged
But I can't complain
Sometimes the temptation is enough

CHANCES

I smell your hair
But the feeling is gone
No longer holding hands,
I want to find you again

I watch you sleep
I wake you up so we can talk
So, we have a chance
I want to understand

MY OTHER HALF

It will take a special person to love me
They'll have to know my heart is unpredictable
One minute, I can be filled of happiness
Next minute, I can be filled with fear

They'll have to know there are some things I'll never be able to do
Daily activities can be a struggle
Hospitals are an annual routine
Travel is sporadic

My heart has put a lot of limitations on me
However, loving another person isn't one of them
My other half is out there, and they will be my miracle

MY HEART IS ALWAYS ON MY MIND

I put my hand on my chest everyday
My scar is right down the middle
It's a constant reminder of my situation

Breathing is hard in the summer
Activity is limited in the winter

In the hospital,
I hear the same speeches,
I get the same tests,
I take the same drive back home

In school,
Whether I'm walking or sitting in class,
I worry about the next cardiac episode

When I'm with friends,
And want to do what other friends do,
I have to think of myself

Constantly thinking of my health is exhausting

EAR TO MY CHEST

I get into bed and my mother puts her ear to my chest

She listens to my heartbeat

And the sound puts both of us at ease

STAY

My heart broke
You left me
You didn't stay

When we fought the first time, you stayed
When we raised our children, you stayed
When money was tight, you stayed
When I left for war, you stayed

Things happened along the way
A point came when we couldn't stay together

It couldn't last

ONLY HAVE TONIGHT

Sitting at the table,
I'm anxious, waiting for you to show

As the waiter presents a menu,
I see other couples laugh,
I hear clinks of glasses,
And I stare at the front door

Seeing you will be a surprise
I get scared that nothing will be real
Will this mean as much to you as it does me?
I'll know soon enough

The love I could feel for you will be hard to deny

If we don't see each other again,
I'm happy to only have tonight

ONE ON ONE

Dear God,
Take me on a journey
Tell me who you have for me
Cause I'm tired of waiting
Is there someone?

It was hard to get peace of mind
Every moment of hope was a waste of time
If you can hear me,
Can you answer me?

Can't you see the love I can give?

SATISFACTION

Sit down, take a breath, and listen to me
My breaths don't come easy

You think life will cave to your wishes?

You think of the next best thing
Your heart always aches for more
Never satisfied

You never think about us
The ones who fight for air
The ones who fight for a voice
The ones who fight for an identity

Treasure the memories
We are satisfied with just that

LET IT GO

I've been holding this in for awhile
I hope to get the nerve to open up to you

Unsure of what to say,
My mind runs in circles

I begin to speak
You listen
Finally, I can let it go

YOU WISH TODAY WASN'T TODAY

The kids sit in the dark, and they're too young to understand
You explain it to them the best that you can
They saw the pain
But always thought things would change

You lie in bed thinking how it came to this
When the future seems hard to imagine,
And your voice seems hard to hear,
You don't know how much more you can bare

You used to laugh and enjoy the time
Someday, someone will figure out how you really felt inside
You try to confide in each other
And hold on to beautiful memories

You close your eyes
You try to remember out first day
You wish today wasn't today

THE FIRST TIME

I made mistakes
I hold on to the ropes, wishing never to fall
But if it's not you,
I don't want love at all

Sitting by the water, time passes by
I worry about us being alright
If tomorrow will be any better

But seeing you makes it feel like the first time

We were living different lives when I met you,
I thought I had all I needed
And now every day feels like the first time
First time you entered my life

ERASED

Forget about him
When will I capture your mind?
My dreams suddenly turned real
Illusions start to fade
And time starts to move on

Emotions are held on your sleeve
The touch of your hand is where I feel safe
I hope you realize now that we're one
I'll hold you close just in case
Because I'm afraid you'll be erased

Sitting in the sand
Writing our names in the sky
Thinking back to when we were strangers,
We grew closer together over time
The wonder is gone
And my life is yours
You were more than I could foresee
And you show me where I belong

I memorized every line and freckle on your face
Even death couldn't make your heart's love be erased

DISTRACTION

A balloon floats to the sun
A young boy looks up
While a man looks down
There's nothing to be done

Then a sudden outburst draws a crowd's attention
Walking and talking follows

The boy's heart is aching
While his mind is thinking,
Cotton candy is up ahead

Father watches his son's tears turn to a smile
Once the taste hits the boy's lips
The subject is forgotten
The day is saved

TOUCH THE SKY

Once upon a time
There was a boy
Wondering why
If he'll ever find love
Will he find it?
Will he feel it?

The day brought him hope
Cause the love came from you
But in a world of hurt
He wonders what he did
Then he realizes he's just a kid

There it is again
There goes another one
You wish you could have him back
But instead,
Your world just goes black
And now you'll never forget
All the lost time
Not being by his side
Wanting to touch the sky

One day you'll look in the mirror
And try to remember who you used to be
Reaching out a hand
Just feeling the air

YOU SAW ME

Look into my heart
Tell me what you see
I want a memory
I always thought it would be a dream
But you proved me wrong when you saw me

There's something you don't know
I've spend my life waiting
Hoping there was someone out there for me
But the future seemed so far away
Something I couldn't see
You brought it all to me
When you saw me

I believed
That I was Romeo and you were Juliet
And all the stars aligned when we met
The moment was extraordinary
I'm not the kind to be seen
But you saw me

We all want to be loved
But some of us feel not good enough
With eyes of judgment passing our way
I fight through the pain
I'll wait for something good to come along
You'll be the one who saw me
Forever
You're all that I need
Always
I just wanted to be seen
Then with you
I finally was

ECHOES

Just an ordinary day
But all the hope had gone away
Buildings crashed to the ground
As did so many dreams
But we never could say goodbye

Lives lost and children born
Voices of painful cries echo in our minds
Memories fill the air
Even if we weren't there

Waking up to a morning war
Knowing our world was about to change
Nothing compares
Even seeing darkness and no sun
Won't make us forget the one's we love
Their love can never be replaced
The day brought nothing but dying grace

We can't return to before
Can't smile now that they're gone
It's as if the day played with time

Standing still,
Trying to stand strong,
We're never going to see them again
All hope died when we saw the plane

But this wouldn't bring us down
Even our flag stood its ground
Still, nothing would be the same
The echo of their love is all that we keep

REFLECTION

I noticed the world is like a carnival
It's beautiful but strange
A mirror with millions of little cracks

People might view the image different than you
But it's yours that counts

On your last night,
You hope to have no regrets
You want God to whisper in your ear
Have Him tell you he loves you

It's now what you should care about
Now that you have control
The reflection looking back at you shows nothing but truth

Now that you walk this unpredictable line,
Now is when you should care about time

THE WEDDING DRESS

I'm sitting in a store, waiting
Hanging
Trying to shimmer and out sparkle the rest
It may be days or even years before it's my turn
Stuck on the row of plastic covered gowns
I'm white for a reason
I hold purity and loyalty within my fabric
I have potential to be the center of attention

Losing patience,
I feel like I'm growing old, grey, and dingy
Please try me on
I don't want to lose my sparkle

Is it going to be today?
Finally, I'm chosen
A woman tries me on
She says she feels special because of me
I shine and brighten up from her smile
She's glowing
That's it, she sheds a tear of joy
Just looking at my beauty makes her cry

If My Heart Could Talk

As I see the church full of color, happiness, and life,
I stick to the woman like I'm hugging her
The warmth from my fabric makes her comfortable
All eyes are on us

It's over and done already
She pulls me off
I try to ignore what's next
I must return to the loneliness
I'm placed in a box
No contact with the woman who changed my life
And I changed hers
All I have is the memory

Years go by
I see my first gleam of light
I get excited
A young woman touches me
She's similar, yet different from the last one
I still look beautiful to her

I'm out of the box
I get that feeling again
The feeling when I give someone the chance to shine

I will always be
I'm a special part of someone's life
Even for a little while
Forever in pictures
I will always be treasured

GRASS

Sunlight hits me, I reach and stretch
Rain hits me, I'm nourished
I'm vulnerable
Open to all elements of life

When it's winter, I'm cold longing to feel warm
When it's summer, I'm happy for a breeze
And when it hits spring, I feel like I'm alive again
Seeing the bright sky for the first time

Day by day, I can't freely move,
I only sway with the wind
I long for a life of freedom, but it'll never happen
Instead I'm here to live a life, set
With the hustle and bustle of life around me

When someone steps on me, I'm wounded
When cut, I'm hurt, but I stay embedded strong

I wonder what the blade next to me thinks of himself?
He's me, just another one of me

Grass is like life
The roots go deep
Unforgiving trials daily
Again, and again
Beautiful to see when cared for
Keeps growing, flourishing, living

We are all blades of grass
It takes all of us together
Behold life
So, if you think about it, we can never die

Has anyone admired us today?

I'M AFRAID OF YOU

I'm afraid of you, I'm afraid of me
Tell me when I can come out
I'm afraid of you, I'm afraid of me
Tell me when you've erased all your doubt
My heart is open, but it's not like yours
But it was you who went through the door
But I stand back
Cause I'm afraid of you

I'm afraid of you
We fell in love
Not knowing what it would bring
It was a mystery
Trying to pick truth amongst the lies
But the reality is, this is me
No turning back
But I'm afraid of you

I'm afraid of you, I'm afraid of me
Tell me when I can come out
If you like me, why can't I see?
I try to reach for your hand
Hope you're there
Cause I'm afraid of you

It's hard living with a scar on your chest

I'm afraid of you
I'm afraid of hurting
I'm afraid of causing hurt
I'm afraid of being invisible

But you're here
And now
All I fear is losing you

YOUNG LOVE

Young love, and the day is good
Hearts are jumping and dreams come alive
Young love comes and goes
Your heart aches, but I won't let you disappear
I'm here

A time
When you get all that you want
Since you're mine
I'll help you fly
Yes, fly
Nothing will hurt you while I'm at your side

Young love changes you fast
Hope it'll last
Birds are singing, and I wouldn't take anything back now
My heart's jumping, and my dreams came alive
Please don't leave and say goodbye

Young love, and the day is good
At last the world can see
I'm not going to leave

REWIND

Remember when we were young?
Walking down the aisle, you said I was an angel
You said you loved me, and I was yours
But that was too long ago
Many of the feelings that were once there have died
And only the memories survived

From the outside looking in,
It all looks great
But no one knows of the mistakes we've made
Don't know about you,
But it gets harder to believe how we feel
I'm losing the will the fight for us
Just want you by my side
Can we just rewind?

Things went wrong, but there's nothing I regret
But the end is near

Tell me
Did you hope for everything you have?
Is the grass greener on the other side?
Cause my heart is turning black
I'm waiting for you, but it won't last
Nothing last forever

Now, I'm moving on with only memories in my mind

Ready to say goodbye
But do you want to try again?
Do you want to conquer time?
We can
But only if first
We rewind

YOU HAVE MY HEART

The sun rises but you feel grey
Your heart's broken
But the feelings won't go away
You found me
Then you cut me so deep
This is something neither of us could see

You had my heart
Took a piece and broke it apart
I try to mend it as I watch you leave me
The nights are hard, and days are gloomy
But I'm up for another shot
Deep inside I know you're all I need
You have my heart, broken or not

Put so much thought into the beginning
You're the one I choose
Cause you're too important to lose
Feelings I had with you
No other could compare
And I love you a lot
You have my heart, broken or not

Forgiving mistakes takes time
But your heart breaks, and so does mine

I'M NOT LEAVING

You touched my heart
I felt like I was the only one who mattered to you
It took time for me to believe it

So, no matter what,
I'm not leaving

I'm happy when you're next to me
When you're gone, I'll be grieving
No need to worry
I'll give unconditionally

Through the good and bad,
I'm not leaving

A BEAUTIFUL PLACE

I want to go somewhere

Mountains and rivers touch
Children feel loved
Words turn to action
Tears turns to smiles
Fears turn to courage
A walk turns to a run

That would be a beautiful place

WRITE

Remember when we had our dreams?
We didn't know the words of our life
But I'll always remember
The look in your eyes

The Earth disappeared beneath my feet
All you did, all you said, it was fate
You're all that I love
Now I can't wait to write

Sitting down, I think ahead
I love these thoughts
I'm stuck with doubts and fears
But there's a constant in my life
And it's you
You're my muse

Everything's clear
I just want to sit down
And write

PHOENIX

Love's like a phoenix
It causes burns but shows us prowess
Hearts are broken but never too late to fix

It's the philosophy we all believe
That love conquers all
It's justified
Shows neglect but never dies

You see love start to form and then watch it cease
Hating yourself for holding a piece
Learn that dreams are just dreams
And they're not as great as they seem

Love's like a phoenix
It withers but can rise in the most unexpected
moments

THE ROAD TO YOU

I know that you build the walls
And you're hurting now
The road was hard, but I made it through
I take everything and learned from the wrong
All so I could get back to you
But the distance made everything go bad
I close my eyes to not face the truth

The road to you will remind me of my mistake
We can make memories as we go

I know the pain we feel is my fault
The road to you hasn't been easy
But you showed me a piece of me I couldn't see
Now it has one heartbeat

Silence eventually forms words
And hearts tend to mend
Winter turns to spring, and pain turns to love
I thank you for knowing I was enough
Present turns to past, and the road to you will never end

HEALING

All the days we created
Meant so much
The memories never faded
Rings have lost their meaning

I thought we would last forever

My heart turns red when you walk in
Anger, hurt
We were met with hard times
Left heartbroken

Now I want to know
Where have you been?
Time has passed
I have softened
I'm healing

We can say we dived in too deep
But neither of us could see how life would be

I thought we would last forever

We never could apologize
We couldn't stay
No hard feelings
I'm healing

HUMAN

I don't want it to be an intrusion
But love is an illusion

I hope before you break my heart
You give me the chance to fix yours
Time goes fast, and it goes slow
But I don't want a minute unless I know you're with me

The walls you put up are keeping me out
But I hold my breath
In hopes of seeing you again
I'm sorry for the pain

I'm just human

The memories come back like a wave
And I don't want to run
I count the hours to when we can move ahead
The time apart has made me stronger

I'm just human

If you take my hand and go into the moonlight
I promise we'll be alright
I know you're hurt but keep on walking
Just stand on the bridge and meet me halfway
You won't regret the choice you make
I won't leave you out in the rain
I hope you stay

DEPENDENT

I had a lot
A lot on my mind
Lying here thinking of you
I can't think of anything else
I hurt to have you
Forgetting everything else
Waiting for you
You're the fix

Looking down at the mirror on the table
My reflection is all I see
I can't stop

You never let me down
You always pick me up
When I'm sick
You make me forget everything that's bad
You're the fix
To all the demons

Every thought I have is of you
Little did I know that I would depend on you this much
Calling to me
You have to be mine
Now our lives are intertwined

I have to let you go before I die

DRUG OF CHOICE

WHEN MY HEART IS ACHING,
AND I NEED AN ESCAPE,
I DON'T RESORT TO ALCOHOL
I GO TO THE MOVIES

SPEECHLESS

Like a period at the end of a sentence,
When air escapes my lungs,
I stop speaking

I'VE GROWN

I had dreams back then
Making them happen on my own
Friends were hard to find and hold

No one knows my secrets
There's nothing left for you
I've moved on and turned over every stone

I've grown

You look in the mirror feeling sorrow
And I've become strong
You might think I'm alone,
But you couldn't be more wrong

I've grown

Eyes were closed, opened, and you were gone
I saw the sun in reach, and I didn't need you to depend on
You were gone
And the pain didn't carry through
I don't need you
You broke my heart, and that's not a friend
But I think of how you've been

ACCEPTANCE

Every man goes through sickness and woes
Contrition can be profound
I know because I know
Pain disappears
Love never goes

The things we lost, we will never forget
But we'll be able to walk away from it
We must accept the past
If we want our hearts to mend

CIVIL

Coffee shops
Parks
Bars
Places where love can start

Lies
Distance
Silence
Is how love can end

Let's take a walk down memory lane
And forget the pain
Say what's on our minds
No judgement, just honesty
We think of our future
Where do we go from here?
We stop at a good point of resolution
We agree to be civil

SIMPLICITY

I see lights
I see fame
But no matter what, I can say I'll remember the days
Days when mornings came without expectations
Days with simple changes
But my mind runs wild with creation

All our dreams go through nasty weather
No need to get upset
The light at the end of the tunnel gets lighter with every step
Time seems slow
We look back and wish we could rewind

The future is as open as the sea
Doesn't mean your future is a guarantee
Life takes turns and has many years to go
Enjoy the sights
Enjoy the pain
Enjoy the pace

FEARLESS

Truthfully,
It's time to see
The man I want to be
And I can't go back
The one you knew has faded in front of you
But from sandboxes to wedding rings,
Days went on, and I borrowed everything

With no fears,
I take the wheel
Every step I take is my choice
From a child to an adult, I'm ready to leave
My life and death are sealed

REMEMBER OUR LIFE

I know it's hard to vision an end
If you knew my story, I wouldn't know where to begin
Death hit me early on
Friends were mean and love was hard to believe in
It was always if and never when

Then time slowed down and showed it to me
And I started living once you found me
I can see all the pain made sense
And all I can say is if you want to be mine
Just please remember our life

Future was grey
Hope was gone
And love was the piece I'd thought I'd never have
Now, hear my heartbeat
I feel so alive
But if you can't,
Promise you'll remember our life

Love comes with joy, and love comes with pain
But after the tears are shed
After the years of strife
When I'm gone
Please remember our life

THAT'S LIFE

We put our hearts on the line
With love taking a long time
To come
Some get it early
And it's a worry
For some
We take the joy and pain it brings
The memories and the mistakes
Cause all we want is to be here
In our golden years

I know you from around
You lifted me off the ground
I had a star in the palm of your hand
But watched it fall
The dreams we made started to fade
And space between us began to grow
But in the end,
I regret nothing at all
Pain strikes our hearts
Then light starts to shine
That's life

I don't want to be dead weight
Still want you here until dawn
The pain is throbbing, and I'm searching for a cure
But with life going on, I know love is never unsure

NEAR DEATH

Driving down the road, I reach the top of a hill
I grab the steering wheel
It's like the front bars of a roller coaster
Panic sets in
When I come to the bottom, I still can't breathe
This is different, I know it is

One hands on my chest and the others on the wheel
Cars are close, but I don't think of crashing
I strain my eyes, focusing on my breath
As I pull over, I nearly hit a sign
I lay in agony as my vision goes white
I have memories of my life
I get ready to say goodbye and hello
Goodbye to my mom and hello to my grandfather

Then my heart slows down
I regain my focus before returning home
The next six months left me traumatized

MATURE

I grew up knowing I wasn't like everyone else
I acted younger than my actual age
I've been emotionally stunted since a teenager
I can never grow to my full potential
My mind tries but my heart is a leash, stopping me
I'm an easy target for people to bully
Like a turtle, I've hid in my shell for years
I want to come out
I want to be a lion
Ruler of my own life
I start by picking up the broken pieces

CONTENT

You forgot who you were
You were my answer
For everything

Now, you're not a part of my life
Where are you going?
You really don't know

We separate
I'm desperate
Two halves
I'm never whole again
I was not his answer

MEANING OF LOVE

Here's a love story of a girl and a boy

He got on one kñee and presented a ring
Not knowing what the future would bring

Her hug was his world
Her dream of a man
All they had was a simple plan

She was twenty-two with her man so strong and kind
Each had thoughts of children on their minds

A child born, and it was clear to see,
They quickly learn what the meaning of love would be

The baby's heartbeat began to cease
Then appeared a vision, an angel of peace

A Savior's light came into view
They knew love when he made it through

All their hearts beating as one
They know in a moment it all could be gone

Everything is possible with help from above
Now they all know a baby's life is the meaning of love

LOVE LEFT OVER FOR ME

Once upon a time,
You had insecurities
You thought no one could climb your wall
But to see where we are,
We have it all
The years have been good to us
Through temptation and different dreams
It so happens life is harder than it seems

Take care of the petals of the wind
Cause if you don't, it will all come to an end
Take care of yourself first, and I'll be next
Life goes on, and we'll be better than you expect
I hope you see the person you used to see
If you have any love left over for me

The past is done and the future, I'll make do
I'll give you some time while you clear your mind
In the meantime, I'll do the best I can
But no matter what's meant to be,
Hope you'll always have love left over for me

A CAT AT A WINDOW

A cat at a window
He's curious
He longs to leave his four walls
The only way to see the world is by his owner

The door opens with the smell of dew
Then sunlight pierces the room
Fireflies and rain drops come into view
He sees his chance to be free
Dashing for the road on a squirrel's tail,
Adrenaline and excitement lets him not fail

His paws touch the driveway
His fur blows in the wind
The world belongs to him
Strolling down the streets
Hiding in grass
Predator searching for prey
He soaks up the day

Moonlight brings new company
Making new friends
Avoiding his enemies

Thoughts of home aren't far from his mind
He is now ready to have his owner by his side
The four walls around him until tomorrow

He was a cat at a window
Once perched,
Now he dreams of his adventures lying on his pillow

A CHILD'S WONDER

A girl plays hopscotch
A boy plays ball
Neither know of pain at all
They're filled with glee,
Unaware of parental eyes
The cruelty of the world has not yet entered their minds

I wonder who will cry first?
The girl?
The boy?

Whoever it is, I wish them each peace afterwards
Parents can smother their offspring in their arms
Sing, recite fairytales, and give them treats

Childhood should be a matter of fun,
Not despair
But in times of need,
One has to wonder,
Who will care?

COUNTING

A cat has nine lives
A spider has eight legs
A rainbow has seven colors
A Star of David has six sides
A hand has five fingers
A year has four seasons
A genie has three wishes
A dance has two partners
A life has one you

REALITY

We hear the vortex like a plane engine
Chaos erupts before hiding
The closet is small and silence is loud
The doorknob is our only solace
Our home is standing with little damage
We're lucky beyond comprehension

Trees and glass cover the road
Neighbors come out one by one
Red Cross and police were helping hands
The calm after the storm
Mother Nature destroyed lives and spared others
A newfound respect brings relation
Message for other victims
You're not alone

A MOTHER'S JOY

Two children in a field of daises
One older than the other
A mother has both her babies at her side
The incredible scene was one to remember
She takes the shot to steal time
The innocence

Her kids go run and play
They laugh
They watch each other
One tumbles into a bed of petals
The other stands with a smile
Pointing up at clouds soon turns to a game

Realizing how small they are in this vast space
Eyes wide open
Embracing the Earth and time
She stares
The colors, the smells, the memory

A field of flowers
Nature's little house in a giant universe
Her children present her with a bouquet as a gift
It tugs at her heart

A mother's life is whole when her babies laugh
It makes her smile and fill with joy

PAPER AND PEN

People know words are the way of communication
But paper and a pen are the way to expression
We put one's heart in a letter
Each are instruments made for a reason
Using them when we can't speak
If paper and a pen were to go,
Try as we might,
Love wouldn't be true unless it's with ink

FRIENDSHIP

A friend is a shoulder
A friend is a voice of reason
It can be real or not
A friend is a friend who treats you like one
And if they don't, that's when you need to be done

IF MY HEART COULD TALK

If my heart could talk
It would say this

I'm complex but asked for only simple things
I was blue wishing to be pink
Having magic hands touch me was a gift

Going back and forth between beating and stillness
I needed to choose so my human body could rest
From the size of a walnut to a fist, I've been through hell
Every birthday, I'm happy to keep beating for another year

Every time I go fast, I want to scream
I'm sorry for giving my host difficulties
I thank him for knowing what's right for me
The tests I go through make me feel nurtured
No genetics or pedigree is the root of my cause
The scar above me is a zipper to the outside world
I'm a part of an exclusive club

I want to have a friend or a partner who understands me
I'm alone working out life's obstacles
I'm scared of the future
Scared of not living to my full potential

Even with my limitations
If my heart could talk
It would say it's happy
It would say it loves this world

THERAPY

Therapy is a place to let yourself go
Once you leave,
A new version of you emerges that will want to stay

LOVE FADES

We say we'll love each other until death do us part
But years have made us see one another differently

Once partners
Now roommates
I pull the covers over myself
And close my eyes
You do the same
Without a word

Love can be enchanting, happy
Painful, ugly, healing, or beautiful

Silence is a killer of love

FAMILY

My favorite part of arguing with you is knowing when we're done,
We'll still love each other

CONTROL

You molded me into the perfect person,
And you still weren't happy
I broke out of the clay and moved forward
Into who I wanted to be
And that makes you sad
But I'm happy
With no reason to look back,
I'm now in control

REGRET

Sometimes,
We are angry at the person we love
But when they're gone,
We regret being angry at them at all

REJECTION

I open my heart and you shut me out

DREAM STATE

I hear my heartbeat constantly
I hear my breathing slow down
I fall asleep
And silence comes

MY HEART'S LIKE YOURS

A heart is a muscle
It pumps blood
It breaks
It heals
It beats after eighteen days in a woman's womb
It goes still in the end
It carries loved ones around
It can attack the body
It burns
It opens to the world
It takes risks
It wants to be guarded
It wants to find the key to unlock its love
It can be good or bad

My heart's like yours
It's just different

STRANGER

You give all your attention to someone,
You forget to give it to yourself
Then one day,
When you look in the mirror,
You see a stranger

INTROSPECTION

We promise to meet each other halfway in times of need
But eventually,
Only one of us is willing to walk across the bridge
Staring down a vacant road,
We realize, standing alone, we're the strong one

TOXIC FRIENDSHIP

We look at a ball and chain as an enemy
A chore we don't want to have
Carrying it with us through life
But once we can run from it,
It's like losing a friend

THE BEST ACTRESS IN THE WORLD

Sitting in a room and knowing someone's missing, hurts
The chair is empty, but her ghost is as real as a kiss
Rumors swirl about the cause of death
Only to learn it was her own doing
Friends come together
Cry, embrace, and curse

No one knows what's inside someone's mind
She was the best actress in the world
Smiling
Only to be damaged behind the mask
She was the brightest one on stage
But she drew the curtain on her own production
Even in the end, the show must go on

MALARKEY

The more you talk,
The louder you get,
The less I hear

PRIDE

A man's shoulders are broad
So are a woman's hips
We all grow up wondering,
Which gender we'd like to kiss?
It's confusing for some,
Straight forward for others
Scared to disappoint,
We swallow our pride
Defending ourselves with a lie
Deep down we know the truth
And it shows on our face
Day after day we get tired
We jump off the tightrope into a safety net

Man, woman, black, white, gay, straight
All humans walk on the same Earth
And deserve to share a life with their own soul mate

DEFIANCE

I don't make my father proud
I'm the football star who wants to be benched
My mother is the same way
I'm a sorority girl who wants to abandon her sisters
I'm his son who must follow in his footsteps to be a man
I'm her daughter who she raises to be as pretty as her
Like father, like son
Mother and daughter bonding
For life

What about mine?

What if I told my father I hated football?
What if I told my mother I hated makeup?
I'm making my own rules

If I walk off the field,
I'll stand tall
If I wear jeans instead of a dress,
I'll fall back on my dignity
I won't be influenced by other voices
I'll take on the world myself

SELF-SABOTAGE

The world is my enemy
So, I grab a friend
One that I can depend on
He gets under my skin sometimes
It stings for a minute,
But I can spend the whole day with him

Then after years of being together,
He begins killing me
The demon in disguise
Convincing me I'll be okay
Having only myself to blame
The choices I made
Started and ended with him

FAMILIAR SOUND

I heard a song in my head as I slept
It was you singing to me
When I wake up, the bed is empty
I smile because the house is full of your voice
Its' s the most beautiful sound I know

INTERRUPTION

Death is on everyone's mind
But with a heart like mine,
It was a near reality
I was what you'd call a blue baby
Not sad, but lifeless
It creeps into my subconscious
And when air escapes me, it's my only thought
Nothing else matters in those moments
My beautiful life is interrupted

Interrupted by scary, heavy darkness
Until breath comes back,
I feel like I'm alone, falling
Nobody or nothing exist except me
I'm screaming for help on the inside
The scream comes out as slow speech

Darkness turns to color
I go on with life
And I prepare for the next interruption
And it could be worse
Who knows?
I don't

REALIZATION

Someone hurt you
You sit in the dark feeling worthless
Deep inside, you know you' re not
You have no choice but to believe the lie
Hope for a better future is sucked from your mind

Like a leech

In the beginning, you hate the state you' re in
Staring at yourself in the mirror in pain,
You have no explanation for how you got this far
Suicide could' ve been your end

You realize the leech is the bully, not you
You look it in the eyes
It' s hungry for fear,
Intimidation, and superiority
You start to see behind the mask
You blame it for making you the way you did,
Yet you also thank it
You remember how it changed your self-perception

DANCING WITH PURPOSE

I'm a ballet dancer on a stage
The audience sees an elegant and remarkably talented performer

I didn't choose this
It was chosen for me
I had no say
I've spent my life feeling hostile

What I want is happiness
But my heart is black as coal
Preventing anyone from unlocking its love
Even me

Now I use dance as an escape though
Hoping it will numb my pain
I'm scared of my own reflection
Hope one day it'll change
I will dance for love and happiness

I'm dancing with purpose
Perfection anticipated
I smile because that's what is expected
They see perfection on stage, but it's all an act
I feel fragile and flawed
I'm breakable

I'm a fish in a bowl rather than a beautiful swan
If the glass cracks, my world will be gone

Only if I could see myself as they see me
I see a tortured soul
It's easier and safer to hide behind the performance
That way I survive

NUISANCE

It must be hard to know when you're with her,
I'm still on your mind

HAND-ME-DOWNS

The stories you read when I was a child have stayed with me into adulthood
Now I'm writing this to read to mine

UNDERSTANDING

We all strive to be normal
Until you learn we're all different for a reason,
You'll never be happy

ONE HUNDRED AND EIGHTY

You fill my mind with thoughts I know aren't true
But they're with me for so long I believe them
Once I heal, I block out everything you convinced me of

QUESTIONING

I don't know what I want
I hate that I don't know myself
I am with a person and wake up in their bed
Feeling like I made a mistake,
I only have more questions

POWER STRUGGLE

You push me down, and I keep getting up
You're using all your strength in anger to break me
Your strength weakens as mine stays the same

DOUBLE STANDARD

The criticism we give men make them feel unworthy of certain things
The support we give women make them feel worthy of something better
Men and women are the same
We bleed
We love
We grieve
We fight
We heal
We hide
We share
We fall
We judge
We accept
We die
We're both human
What's the difference?

THANKFUL

Loving you was the greatest gift of my life

Losing you was the greatest loss

But it was still a gift

Not everyone has a love like we had

So, for that, I'm thankful

ROLE REVERSAL

You told me to go, I left
You still wanted control
When you wanted me back, you did everything so I would stay
I still left

DIRTY

When we first meet someone,
We put our best foot forward
Then life throws dirt on us
We must drag our feet through mud
But in the end, we clean them off and smile at each other

QUESTION ABOUT LOVE

Do people make love in the dark or the light?
Is there a wrong way?
I don't know

INFINITY

The love I have for you is like outer space
It never ends
And no gravity is needed to hold it in my heart

HINDSIGHT

Over time, you will thank the person who made you so angry

MANIPULATION

We are each our own person,
Yet we allow people to turn us into another

CROSSROADS

When your mind is telling you one thing,
And your heart is telling you another,
You choose
Hopefully they are in sync
But that's how choices are made

MOTHER'S INSTINCT

When a child tastes their mother's milk,
They feel nurtured
When a child smells their mother's hair,
They feel comforted
When a mother sees her child smile,
Her face glows
When a mother hears her child cry,
Her heart aches
When a mother touches her child's hands,
Her love is real
When a mother and child are together,
Everything makes sense

ENOUGH

I look for someone to love
But found out I didn't have to search that far
I had enough to fill my heart

TUG-A-WAR

Your mind and heart are screaming
But no words come out
Anxiety is a tug-a-war
War between desire and fear

Always fighting
Always retreating

After years, a tug-a-war doesn’t seem hard
Anxiety becomes the norm

Your mind and heart stop screaming
You drop the rope and walk away
Desire wins
The horizon looks hopeful
The thing pulling you forward is life’s unknowns
No more fear

NEW BEGINNING

Every tear I've shed, I did in my bed
My pillow was an ocean of painful memories,
But I washed the linens,
And now everything's clean
I'm ready to face another day

UNPREDICTABLE

A boy is watching a girl dance
He walks over to join her
It's a moment they share
They will grow and fall in love
But don't know how their life will go

ALIVE

You set the world on fire
Then I came along and put it out
It made me feel alive

This scar on my chest is the best trait I have
It shows my strength
Shows I'm alive

I told you to sit down and take a breath
I can do the rest on my own
Don't worry about me
I will thrive
I'm alive

AWAKENING

My body is my own
I stand naked in front of you and love every part of me
The curves,
The scars,
The hair

I was insecure
Now I'm sure
I'm ready to create music
My body is an instrument that's never been played
I let your fingers do the work
They move slowly,
As if they're exploring new territory
A duet is better than a solo
Two people hitting every note
Free to go up and down as we please
It's my first time
Who cares if I'm off key?
I'm awake

LITTLE RED WAGON

A boy rides in a little red wagon in a field of flowers
Hands in the air, he cheers
With the Earth beneath him, he looks over the side and smiles
He then stares at the horizon, imagining where he'll end up
In his mind, he's riding to a castle
The little red wagon is his horse
The field of flowers is his own magical land
He's a king

CIRCUMSTANCE

Any person can be a bully or a victim

No one is immune from hurt

Be better than a bully

MY VOICE

The minute I put a pen in my hand,
I found my voice

LETTER TO PETER

God chose you to have a special heart
I know it may seem unfair
Why does yours have to be different?
But I promise you'll be able to handle it

The scar on your chest is a symbol of your struggles
It shows your strength
It gives you character
God believes you can become the man you want to be,
I want you to believe it too

In this way we're alike, so I understand
I understand any doubts you have about yourself
I understand the challenges you will face
I understand the desire to feel normal
I understand you had no choice
I understand you don't want to be special
But you are

Every birthday you celebrate will be a gift
Every heartbeat is a blessing
You'll be faced with new challenges
But you'll have love around to support you

Your heart is different
You're special
Embrace it
I want you to know God loves you
And wants to live the life you dream for yourself
You have a chance to share your view of the world
To show people what it could say
If your heart could talk

MICHAEL'S WORLD

We all live in the same world

Everyone sees their world differently

This is mine